Other mini books in this series:
Book Lovers Quotations
Cat Quotations
Golf Quotations
Love Quotations
Music Lovers Quotations
Teddy Bear Quotations

Published simultaneously in 1992 by Exley Publications Ltd in Great Britain and Exley Giftbooks in the USA.
First published in Great Britain in 1991 by Exley Publications Ltd.
Copyright © Helen Exley 1991
Second, third and fourth printings 1992
Fifth printing 1993
ISBN 1-85015-269-1
A copy of the CIP data is available from the British Library on request.

Designed by Pinpoint Design Company.
Picture Research: Alexander Goldberg and James Clift.
Edited by Helen Exley.
Printed in Hungary.

Picture Credits: The Bridgeman Art Library: Cover, 21 (Sir Alfred Munnings, 'The Poppy Field') 24-25 (Wright Barker, 'On the Way Home'), 31 (Gerhard Munthe, 'At the Farm'), 46-47 (George Clauson, 'Homewards'); Christie's Colour Library: 7, 12-13, 48; e. t. archive: 9; Explorer Archives: 32-33; Mary Evans Picture Library: 10, 19, 29, 34; Fine Art Photographic Library Ltd: 14-15; Folio: 5; Scala: 17, 23, 26-27, 36-37, 39, 41, 43, 45, 50-51, 53, 55, 57, 58-59, 61.
Acknowledgements: Extract by Jackie Croome from *The English and Their Horses* by Libby Purves and Paul Heiney is reprinted by permission of The Bodley Head. Extract from *Silver Sand and Snow* by Eleanor Farjeon, published by Michael Joseph, is reprinted by permission of David Higham Associates. Extract from *Pulling Punches* by Paul Heiney is reprinted by permission of the publisher, Methuen (London), and A. P. Watt Ltd. Extract from *The Royal Horse of Europe* by Sylvia Koch is reprinted by permission of the publisher, J. A. Allen & Co. Ltd. Excerpt from *August 1914* by Alexander Solzhenitsyn. Translation copyright © 1989 by The Bodley Head, and Farrar, Straus and Giroux, Inc. Reprinted by permission of The Bodley Head, and Farrar, Straus and Giroux, Inc.

Exley Publications Ltd, 16 Chalk Hill, Watford, Herts WD1 4BN, United Kingdom.
Exley Giftbooks, 359 East Main Street, Suite 3D, Mount Kisco, NY 10549, USA.

*H*ORSE
QUOTATIONS

A COLLECTION OF
BEAUTIFUL PICTURES AND THE
BEST HORSE QUOTES

❖

EDITED BY
HELEN EXLEY

EXLEY

"A horse is the projection of peoples' dreams about themselves - strong, powerful, beautiful - and it has the capability of giving us escape from our mundane existence."
PAM BROWN, b. 1928

❖

"There is something about the outside of a horse that is good for the inside of a man."
SIR WINSTON CHURCHILL (1874-1965)

❖

"The sight of [that pony] did something to me I've never quite been able to explain. He was more than tremendous strength and speed and beauty of motion. He set me dreaming."
WALT MOREY

❖

"In riding a horse, we borrow freedom."
HELEN THOMSON, b. 1943

❖

What delight
To back the flying steed that challenges
The wind for speed! – seems native more of air
Than earth! – whose burden only lends him fire!
Whose soul in his task, turns labour into sport!
Who makes your pastime his! I sit him now!
He takes away my breath – He makes me reel!
I touch not earth – I see not – hear not – all
Is ecstasy of motion!
JAMES SHERIDAN KNOWLES

❖

"A canter is a cure for every evil."
BENJAMIN DISRAELI (1804-81)

❖

Here's to you, Stocking and Star and Blaze!
You brought me all that the best could bring –
Health and Mirth and the Merriest Days
In the Open Fields and the Woodland Ways –
And what can I do in return but sing
A song or two in your praise!

WILL H. OGILVIE

❖

"The air of heaven is that which blows
between a horse's ears."
ARABIAN PROVERB

❖

"Men are better when riding, more just and
more understanding, and more alert and more at
ease and more under-taking, and better knowing
of all countries and all passages; in short and
long all good customs and manners cometh
thereof, and the health of man and of his soul."
EDWARD PLANTAGENET, DUKE OF YORK

❖

"God forbid that I should go to any heaven
where there are no horses."
R. B. CUNNINGHAM-GRAHAM

❖

"We have almost forgotten how strange a thing it is that so huge and powerful and intelligent an animal as a horse should allow another, and far more feeble animal, to ride upon its back."

PETER GRAY, b. 1928

❖

"Far back, far back in our dark soul the horse
prances . . . The horse, the horse! The symbol of
surging potency and power of movement,
of action . . ."
D. H. LAWRENCE (1885-1930)

❖

"We have been companions now for centuries. I
rode you in high festival to the Parthenon and to
the edges of the unknown world under the
Shadow of the Eagles. Together we re-took the
Holy Places, endured the horrors of the
crossing to the Crimea. You took me to
adventure and to love. We two have shared
great joy and great sorrow.
And now I stand at the gate of the paddock,
watching you run in an ecstasy of freedom,
knowing you will return to stand quietly,
loyally, beside me."
PAM BROWN, b. 1928

❖

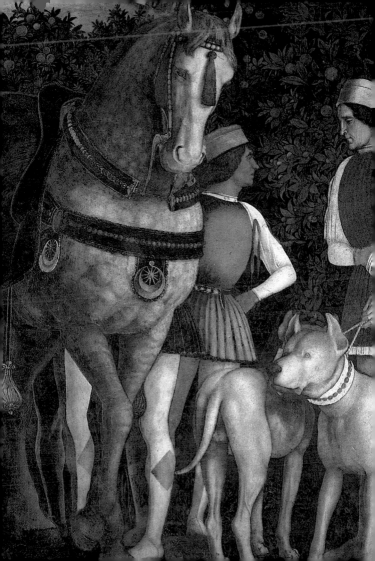

"A horse is worth more than riches."
SPANISH PROVERB

❖

"Gipsy gold does not chink and glitter.
It gleams in the sun and neighs in the dark."
SAYING OF THE CLADDAGH GIPSIES OF GALWAY

❖

"Thou shalt be for Man a source of happiness
and wealth; thy back shall be a seat of honour,
and thy belly of riches; every grain of barley
given thee shall purchase indulgence
for the sinner."
THE KORAN

❖

"The horse is God's gift to mankind."
ARABIAN PROVERB

"What a creature he was! Never have I felt such a horse between my knees. His great haunches gathered under him with every stride, and he shot forward ever faster and faster, stretched like a greyhound, while the wind beat in my face and whistled past my ears."

ARTHUR CONAN DOYLE (1859-1930)
from "The Adventures of Brigadier Guard"

❖

"As I ride, as I ride,
Ne'er has spur my swift horse plied,
Yet his hide, streaked and pied,
As I ride, as I ride,
– Zebra-footed, ostrich-thighed –
How has vied stride with stride
As I ride, as I ride!"

ROBERT BROWNING
from "Through the Metidja to Abd-el-Kadr"

❖

"Riding turns 'I wish'
into 'I can'."
PAM BROWN, b. 1928

❖

My horse with a mane made of short
rainbows.
My horse with ears made of round corn.
My horse with eyes made of big stars.
My horse with a head made of mixed waters.
My horse with teeth made of white shell.
The long rainbow is in his mouth for a bridle
and with it I guide him.
When my horse neighs,
different-coloured horses follow.
When my horse neighs,
different-coloured sheep follow.
I am wealthy because of him
Before me peaceful
Behind me peaceful
Under me peaceful
Over me peaceful –
Peaceful voice when he neighs.
I am everlasting and peaceful
I stand for my horse.

from Louis Watchman's version of the Navajo "Horse Story"

"What is this spell which he [Trollope] himself could not 'fathom or understand', and which held him and has held so many men and women through the generations? . . . Why, to the very end, long after they can sit a horse, does something stir them at the smell from merely a stale and rusty box of saddle soap . . . These things are among the beauties of this earth; and they are reinforced by a thousand minor joys – by the schooling of young horses, by the mysteries of oats and bran and bandages, by the quality of leather and melton and cord, by soft, late-August day-breaks and hard, bright mornings of November, by the light on autumn oak leaves and brown furry swamps."

JAMES BOYD, M.F.H.

❖

"I remember the plough horses. Big, beautiful, plodding fellows, I loved them so. Picture the scene: A pale blue morning, glistening at the edges, and a farmer ploughing with his horse-team. A fragile autumn sun glinting on plough and harness. Grey and white seagulls flying over. And the horses. Filled-out, strong-muscled, sleek with sweat, the long fetlock hairs about their hoofs creamed in a flurry of endeavour as the plough slices deep in the earth, cutting straight and true behind them. And the clean, crumbling earth lying in a dark ribbon by the fresh furrow beside the farmer's striding feet."

ROY BOLITHO

❖

"With flowing tail and flying mane,
Wide nostrils, never stretched by pain,
Mouths bloodless to the bit or rein,
And feet that iron never shod,
And flanks unscar'd by spur or rod
A thousand horses – the wild – the free –
Like waves that follow o'er the sea,
Came thickly thundering on."

LORD BYRON (1788-1824)
from "Marzeppa"

"When he stood trembling with fear before the captor, bruised from falls by the restrictive rope, made submissive by choking, clogs, cuts and starvation, he had lost what made him so beautiful and free. . . . One out of every three mustangs captured in south west Texas was expected to die before they were tamed. The process often broke the spirits of the other two."

J. FRANK DOBI, *from "The Mustang – Wild and Free"*

"An extra pressure, a silent rebuke, an unseen praising, a firm correction: all these passed between us as through telegraph wires."

CHRISTILOT HANSON BOYLEN

❖

"There is no secret so close as that between a rider and his horse."

ROBERT SMITH SURTEES (1803-64)
from "Mr. Sponge's Sporting Tour"

❖

"The rhythm of the ride carried them on and on, and she knew that the horse was as eager as she, as much in love with the speed and air and freedom."

GEORGESS McHARGUE

❖

"A good horse and a good rider are only so
in mutual trust."

H.M.E.

❖

"A horse loves freedom, and the weariest old work horse will roll on the ground or break into a lumbering gallop when he is turned loose in the open."

GERALD RAFTERY
from "The Snow Cloud Stallion"

❖

"It was a great treat to us to be turned out into the home paddock or the old orchard; the grass was so cool and soft to our feet, the air is so sweet, and the freedom to do as we like was so pleasant; to gallop, to lie down, and roll over on our backs, or to nibble the sweet grass. Then it was a very good time for talking, as we stood together under the shade of the large chestnut tree."

ANNA SEWELL (1820-78)
from "Black Beauty"

❖

"Again the early-morning sun was generous with its warmth. All the sounds dear to a horseman were around me - the snort of the horses as they cleared their throats, the gentle swish of their tails, the tinkle of the irons as we flung the saddles over their backs - little sounds of no importance, but they stay in the unconscious library of the memory."

WYNFORD VAUGHAN-THOMAS

"The hooves of the horses!
Oh! witching and sweet
Is the music earth steals from the iron-shod feet;
No whisper of lover, no trilling of bird,
Can stir me as hooves of the horses
have stirred."

WILL H. OGILVIE

❖

"She was not afraid, immediately. The sheer exhilaration of the horse's speed thrilled her, but his strength was ominous. When she looked down she saw his shoulders moving with the smooth rhythm of steam-pistons; she saw his black, shining hoofs thrown out, thudding the hard turf, and felt the great eagerness coming up through her own body. She knew that she could never stop him, if he decided he did not want to stop. She saw the hedge ahead of them, and the first stab of real fear contracted her stomach. She gathered her reins up tight, and pulled hard. It made no difference at all.

'Don't panic,' she thought, but the panic was in her, whether she wanted it or not."

K. M. PEYTON
from "Flambards"

❖

"The ability and intelligence is remarkable . . . Prince was able to walk the length of the furrow, between the growing potatoes, and when he was done you might never guess that he had passed that way, so sure and careful was every footfall."

PAUL HEINEY

❖

"A farmer's horse is never lame, never unfit to go. Never throws out curbs, never breaks down before or behind. Like his master he is never showy. He does not paw and prance, and arch his neck, and bid the world admire his beauties . . . and when he is wanted, he can always do his work."

ANTHONY TROLLOPE

Scores, hundreds of horses are wandering
around, gathering into herds and into twos and
threes, lost, exhausted, bony, but still alive
where they have been able to wrench themselves
free from a team whose other horses have been
killed; some, like our horse, are still in harness,
or dragging a shaft with them,
and there are wounded horses . . .
the undecorated, unnamed heroes of the battle
who for a hundred, two hundred miles have
hauled this artillery, now dead and
drowning in the swamp . . .

ALEXANDER SOLZHENITSYN, b. 1918
from August 1914

❖

"Look back at our struggle for freedom,
Trace our present day's strength to its source;
And you'll find that man's pathway to glory
Is strewn with the bones of a horse."

ANONYMOUS

"In those far-off unmechanized days, suffering by horses in the pursuit of men's bitter quarrels was taken for granted. Horses have died in their unrecorded millions in the service of their country from the first cavalry horses of the Celtiberians, scaling the rocks of Spain and Portugal in support of Hannibal, to the selfless sacrifice of the British horses which galloped undemurring into the Russian guns at Balaclava."

SYLVIA LOCH
from "The Royal Horse of Europe"

❖

"In grateful and reverent memory of the Empire's horses (some 375,000) who fell in the Great War (1914-1918). Most obediently, and often most painfully, they died."

Memorial at Church of St. Jude, London

❖

"Brooks too wide for our leaping, hedges far too high. Loads too heavy for our moving, burdens too cumbersome for us to bear. Distances far beyond our journeying. The horse gave us mastery."

PAM BROWN, b. 1928

❖

"No one who longs for the 'good old days' sighs for the passing of the working horse. Not if he or she loves horses."

MARION C. GARRETTY

❖

"That hoss wasn't built to tread the earth,
He took natural to the air,
And every time he went aloft,
He tried to leave me there."

Anonymous tribute to an unmanageable horse

❖

"He flung himself upon his horse and rode
madly off in all directions."

STEPHEN LEACOCK (1869-1944)

❖

"It takes a good deal of physical courage to ride
a horse. This, however, I have. I get it at about
forty cents a flask, and take it as required."

STEPHEN LEACOCK (1869-1944)
from "Literary Lapses Reflections on Riding"

❖

"A horse is dangerous at both ends and
uncomfortable in the middle."
IAN FLEMING (1908-64)

❖

"I prefer a bike to a horse. The brakes are
more easily checked."
LAMBERT JEFFRIES

"You can tell a horse owner by the interior of their car. Boots, mud, pony nuts, straw, items of tack and a screwed-up waxed jacket of incredible antiquity.
There is normally a top layer of children and dogs."

HELEN THOMSON, b. 1943

❖

"Small children are convinced that ponies
deserve to see the inside of the house."
MAYA PATEL

❖

"The child who ran weeping to you with a cut
finger is now brought home, smiling gamely,
with a broken collar-bone and incredible
contusions – 'it wasn't Jezebel's *fault*, Dad.' "
PAM BROWN, b. 1928

❖

"The daughter who won't lift a finger in the
house is the same child who cycles madly off in
the pouring rain to spend all morning mucking
out a stable."
SAMANTHA ARMSTRONG

❖

"Even an E-type Jaguar looks merely flash beside a really smart pony and trap."

MARION C. GARRETTY

" A horse can lend its rider the speed and strength he or she lacks – but the rider who is wise remembers it is no more than a loan."

PAM BROWN, b. 1928

❖

"Horses do change, you know; a lot of the . . . ponies really give the able-bodied grooms a hard time, but if you put a disabled child or adult on their back they're as gentle as lambs. I don't know what it is: they seem to sense something."

JACKIE CROOME
from "The English and Their Horses"

❖

"To be loved by a horse, or by any animal, should fill us with awe - for we have not deserved it."

MARION C. GARRETTY, b. 1917

❖

"Where in this wide world can [a person] find nobility without pride, friendship without envy or beauty without vanity? Here, where grace is laced with muscle and strength by gentleness confined. He serves without servility, he has fought without enmity. There is nothing so powerful, nothing less violent; there is nothing so quick, nothing more patient."

RONALD DUNCAN
from "To the Horse"

❖

". . . This most noble beast is the most beautiful, the swiftest and of the highest courage of domesticated animals. His long mane and tail adorn and beautify him. He is of a fiery temperament, but good tempered, obedient, docile and well-mannered."

PEDRO GARCIA CONDE, 1685

❖

I must sell my horse because the skies
are snowing,
Nothing in the cupboard, children
crying on the floor.
Never was another horse like him for going;
I must sell my horse to keep the wolf
from the door.
Friend, old friend, the children want their meat,
In another stable you'll have corn to eat.

Once he drew the rake that sent the
green hay flying,
Once he drew the cart that carried yellow corn,
Once I rode my horse because a man was dying,
Once I rode my horse because a child was born.
Friend, old friend, the children want their meat,
In another stable you'll have corn to eat.

ELEANOR FARJEON

❖

"Through the days of love and celebration and joy, and through the dark days of mourning – the faithful horse has been with us always."

ELIZABETH COTTON

"Oh, that ride! That first ride! - most truly it was an epoch in my existence; and I still look back to it with feelings of longing and regret. People may talk of their first love - it is a very agreeable event, I dare say - but give me the flush, and triumph and glorious sweat of a first ride, like mine of the mighty cob . . ."

GEORGE BORROW (1803-81)
from "Lavengro"

❖

"If you have it, it is for life. It is a disease for which there is no cure. You will go on riding even after they have to haul you onto a comfortable wise old cob, with feet like inverted buckets and a back like a fireside chair."

MONICA DICKENS

❖